CLASSROOM SECRETS EVERY TEACHER MUST KNOW

The Guide to Successful Classroom Set Up,
Organization and Management

JOYCELYN RHODES

DICKERSON-REID INTERNATIONAL

Copyright ©2017, 2018 Joyceln Rhodes
The KISS Methods: Classroom Secrets Every Teacher Must Know: The Guide to Successful Classroom Set Up, Organization and Management
Joyceln Rhodes

ISBN: 978-0-692-90659-0
Library of Congress: 2017950566
Completed: 07/27/2017

The copyright belongs solely to the author, Joyceln Rhodes. All rights reserved. No part of this publication may be reproduced, stored in a retrieval system, or transmitted in any form or by any means—for example, electronic, photocopying or recording—without the prior written consent of the author. The author can be contacted at theKISSmethods@gmail.com

Cover & Interior Design by D.E. West - ZAQ Designs

Printed in the United States of America

Dickerson-Reid International

DEDICATION

This book is dedicated to my sons Darnell and Wayne who willingly sacrificed so much, when they were younger even though they really wanted more of my time. Now that they are older, they are my chief motivators and encouragers.
I love you two very with all my heart.

ACKNOWLEDGEMENTS

First and foremost, I would like to thank God, my very, very best friend, who gave me the wisdom and guidance to pursue and complete this book. Had it not been for His grace and favor, this book would not be available. Thousands of teachers would not have the opportunity to explore the options for organizing educational programs with excellence.

I am grateful to my family and friends for continuing to support me even when it seemed as though I had given up. Deborah Pettway, a dear friend who kept asking me, "How far have you gotten on your book?"

Thanks to Senator Dr. Michael Rhett for his numerous notes of encouragement and his honest opinion of this book and to Dr. James Cleveland for his honest critique of this book and the encouragement along the way and for being one of the best principals I have ever had.

And last but certainly not least, Sharon C. Jenkins, The Master Communicator and Literary Midwife for coaching me through this process during trying times in my life. Francisco Blasco one of the happiest professional photographers I know, who stuck with me to produce a fabulous portrait of me for the back cover. DTR Media Group for their social media and website management as well as content production.

TABLE OF CONTENTS

Dedication iii
Acknowledgments v
Introduction ix
How to Use This Book xi

Chapter 1: THE PLAN 1
Chapter 2: THE SETUP 7
Chapter 3: "THE MUSTS" The Beginning 11
Chapter 4: RECORD KEEPING 15
Chapter 5: REPORTS 21
Chapter 6: SCHEDULES 25
Chapter 7: CURRICULUM INTEGRATION 31
Chapter 8: TEACHINGS STYLES 35
Chapter 9: LEARNING STYLES 39
Chapter 10: TESTING 43
Chapter 11: LESSON PLANS 49
Chapter 12: OPEN HOUSE 53
Chapter 13: PARENT CONFERENCES 57
Chapter 14: SPECIAL PROJECTS 61
Chapter 15: FIELD TRIPS 65
Chapter 16: "THE MUSTS" The End 69
Chapter 17: STRESS MANAGEMENT 75

Resources List 79
Bibliography 81

INTRODUCTION

Books on the history, theory and practices of teaching are in abundance in bookstores and libraries. There are excellent textbooks focused on educational best methods used in the undergraduate and graduate programs in colleges and universities. School systems do a great job of introducing teachers to the current policies, procedures, best practices and curriculum. Yet, when teachers step into their classrooms, the reality of preparing for the school year stares them right in the face. What they see is an empty room filled with desks, tables, blank walls and a chalkboard or whiteboard. At this point, it is time to plan, setup, organize and prepare for the school year before any teaching can take place.

The KISS (Keep It Simple Sweetie) Methods: Classroom Secrets Every Teacher Must Know is a simple how-to book designed to direct, train and motivate teachers in the development of a classroom management program that will be advantageous to their overall educational system. It places emphasis on planning, setting up, organizing and managing a successful classroom system.

This step by step guide can be used for individual users, training seminars, college and university mini-courses, educational conferences, charter and pre-school training and more. The KISS Methods also has a comprehensive supplemental resource package that can be found on the website or by emailing us.

This program is conducive to achieving excellence in the classroom and it sets the teacher free to educate the students. The KISS Methods will enhance the total excellence of your students and further enrich the credibility of the school system in which you teach because you will be better equipped for the classroom. Happy Teaching!

HOW TO USE THIS BOOK

Although this book does not have all the answers, it does address many concerns that educators may have on setting up, organizing and managing a successful classroom system. It can be used to help create or re-create (for experienced teachers looking for a different way to manage their classroom management system or remediation for teachers needing assistance with classroom management skills) a method of preparing for each school year. If this book is being used as the text in your college or university, teacher in-service, training or conference course, your instructor will indicate which chapter(s) that are pertinent to your course of study. On the other hand, if you will be using it individually, follow the following three step process.

1. First, read it all the way through the book so that you can take notes of the components that will be of practical use to you.

2. Second, follow along step by step to take advantage of the proven techniques and research.

3. Third, use it as a reference guide when organizing your own classroom management system.

Each chapter contains an encouraging Quote, Objective, Motivation and ends with Diamond Checkpoints for easy reference for the content discussed in each chapter. Within these page you will find a wealth of information that will save you time and energy. It is important for you to understand that there are many ways to organize your educational system and know that the best way to organize your system is the best way for you!

I recommend that you read the book in its entirety before using it as a reference tool because in some chapters there are references to other sections that you may miss. Know that some chapters may take longer to institute than others. In taking the time to get the full effect of The KISS Methods, you will benefit from the added tips, pointers and treasures that are within its pages. Here's to your success!

"Planning is the key to all successes."

CHAPTER 1
THE PLAN

OBJECTIVES
- To develop ideas and practices that will increase teacher effectiveness in the classroom.
- To establish ground rules, routines and procedures for the school year.
- To create and design themes, boards, models and blueprint.
- To set up the curriculum to fit your teaching needs and style.

MOTIVATION
- To plan ahead is to stay ahead. Deciding on key issues before entering the school building, will allow teachers to concentrate on other areas that will need their attention without worrying about where to start or what to do next.

Planning is an essential part of every successful project, especially when educating children. If you fail to plan, it is almost certain that you will not be a success. Plan to succeed and then make any necessary adjustments along the way. It will increase the chances of your program being one of merit and value. To assure that chances for success are great, plan, make decisions and organize your classroom and schedule before you are expected to report for service.

Before school is to open for teacher pre-planning days, you can plan and mentally organize your classroom for the coming school year in the relaxed atmosphere of your home. Completely go through each component of your curriculum and develop a plan that can be implemented in the beginning of the school year that can help you maintain an excellent momentum all year long.

Step 1: Visit your school at least once before teachers are to officially report for work. During the visit, acquire a class list, locate your classroom, sketch the floor plan and be sure to include the wall space, bulletin boards and storage areas. Tour the building to discover where the lunchroom, media center, counselor's office and other rooms are in proximity to your classroom. Obtain copies of teacher's editions of your subject areas or copy the content pages. Also, ask for a copy of the School System and State Objectives for the grade level that you will teach. This way you can become familiar with the progression of these objectives and work on curriculum integration. There will be more on curriculum integration in a later chapter.

Step 2: Establish a theme for the year. Be creative. Choose a theme that will be of interest to the grade and maturity level of the students to whom you will teach. The theme may consist of an animal or cartoon character that is familiar to the younger students, such as "Dora" or a more mature theme such as "The Best is Yet to Come" for older students. It could also be a universal theme, such as "Careers" or a simpler theme for a younger group such as, "My Favorite Animal," "What I Want to Be When I Grow Up" or "My Favorite Super Hero."

Step 3: Write a welcome letter or letter of introduction to parents. When writing this letter, be brief, friendly and to the point. Introduce yourself; give the classroom number, how you can be reached at school and the best time to speak with you directly. Share your expectations for the year and let the parents know what the yearly theme is and about any special events planned that require their attendance. Let them know what your goals are for the school year and share any new policies or protocols that may need to be brought to their attention. This is also a great time to inform parents of the upcoming Open House, PTA/PTO or any other parent support organization meeting. Encourage them to become an active member of the PTA/PTO. End the letter with an enthusiastic conclusion. Remind them that you are looking forward to meeting with them to discuss your plans to provide the best educational program possible for their child.

Step: 4: Design, make and laminate name tags. After the tags are complete, use a permanent marker to write names on the laminated tags. For repeated use or to make corrections, use holding hair spray to remove the permanent marker ink. You may choose to purchases name tags, but remember that you will also need name tags for field trips, for the substitute teacher on days when you are absent from school and for other special events during the year. For these reasons, creating name tags yourself is much more cost effective. To attach the name tags to the students, choose from either of the following options: (1) using a hole puncher, punch one hole in the top or two holes into the top corners of the name tag. Insert yarn, and then place it around each student's neck so that it hangs one inch below the chest. (2) Use safety pins or straight pins to attach the tags. Or, (3) Use Velcro stick-ons to attach the tags. Whichever option you choose, printing the tags ahead will save time.

Step 5: Create bulletin board designs to support the main theme or to support your subject areas. If you choose to create a bulletin board according to the theme, design your artwork focusing on careers that deal with math, science, reading, writing or social studies. Then, after school has been in session for a few weeks, adjust these boards to display student work in the same subjects. Bear in mind bulletin boards are to be changed periodically throughout the school year.

Step 6: Draw a model of how you want your classroom to be set up. Use the sketch that you drew of your classroom when you visited the school. Include teacher's desk, student desks, tables, chairs, bookcases, interest centers, standing charts and items that will occupy floor space. Always allow enough space for maneuverability.

Step 7: Make a list of Audio-Visual (AV) materials that you might use in the classroom. Items such as a television, library books, magazines, a tape recorder and cassette and video tapes, filmstrip projector and films, a computer and computer software, games, CD's and DVD's and other materials and manuals. Having this list available when you go to the Media Center is a time saver. Carry a rolling cart when you go to checkout equipment to help transport the materials back to your classroom.

Step 8: Establish a discipline model, complete with the consequences for each violation. You can make this as simple or as elaborate as you choose. Always remember that simplicity is the key to understanding. Decide which discipline system you will use or you might choose to use a combination of systems. Choose from those learned in college courses or research other models in the Teacher Center Library. After you have established the dos and don'ts, write them on poster board or on chart paper for display in the classroom. Create two hard copies; one for your files and one for each student's folder (you may choose to use it as a requirement for passing). Review the hard copy along with the course syllabus before each reporting period as a checkpoint.

Step 9: Create a daily routine. Start with what is expected of students from the time they walk into the school building, until time for dismissal in the afternoon. Along with the daily routine format, include a classroom procedure model. This model should consist of what is expected when students begin and end a subject, how interest centers will operate, moving around in the classroom, time limits and entering and leaving the classroom. It must also include what to do in case of emergencies, procedures to follow when preparing for lunch or other classroom breaks. How interest centers are to be operated and how completed class work and homework are to be handed in or digitally submitted. Here are a few suggestions proven to help aid the classroom experience. Please freely add other options that are important to you.

Step 10: Create a classroom helpers chart. This step may be of better use to the elementary school teacher and some self-contained middle and high school teachers. Consider such student helpers as Teacher Assistant, Attendance Clerk, Lunchroom Monitors, Line Leader, Pencil Monitor, Current Event Leader, Office Runner, Equipment Monitor or Clean Up Inspector. Determine the process of rotating names and determine how often they will rotate.

Step 11: Visit the Teachers Center. There is a wealth of good information, ideas and materials to choose from. While there, check with the Teacher Center staff to confirm whether or not your school has an established account with them. If they do, you can make and buy materials at your school's expense. You can also make pictures and other items necessary to hang bulletin boards and wall hangings. Be sure to laminate your completed work to preserve it for future use.

Here are a few ideas to help you get started. When it is time for action, you will already have made the final decision on these very important issues. Completing these steps now will save valuable time and energy later. Just think of it, you have completed some of the most important steps in preparing for a successful educational career. Now that you have accomplished these vital pre-planning steps in classroom preparation let's proceed to another phase of preparation for a successful school year.

DIAMOND CHECKPOINTS

Below is a review of The Plan. Check off those steps you have successfully completed as you finish them.

- Establish the yearly theme or motto
- Write a welcome letter or letter of introduction to parents
- Draw, construct or purchase name tags, then laminate for repeated use
- Create bulletin board designs
- Draw a model of the classroom set up
- Write a list of Audio-Visual Equipment, (AV)
- Establish a discipline model
- Create a daily routine
- Create a Classroom Helpers Chart
- Visit the Teachers Center

"Preparedness and organization bring peace of mind."

CHAPTER 2
THE SETUP

OBJECTIVES

- To organize and set up the physical classroom environment.
- To place additional equipment in specific areas for use.
- To set up interest centers.

MOTIVATION

- To help teachers understand that the sooner they physically set up the classroom the better prepared they will be to receive visitors and students before school begins. It would relieve the anxiety of classroom preparedness. Better yet, it would be a definite plus if the classroom were set up prior to the teacher planning days.

There is not much you can do with the basic format of your classroom. However, if you want your students to believe that what you are teaching is important and interesting, you must say it to them in several different ways. By making your classroom as physically attractive as possible, you increase enthusiasm for learning in your students. Explore inexpensive ways of decorating. Plants are always a great source of decorating and they can be educational, as well. Aquariums, terrariums and ant farms are good interest center decor and they also have calming effects on some children. There may even be items in your own home that may enhance the classroom decor. When setting up your classroom, first, bring all items you will need to accomplish the task. This includes materials brought from home, supplies given to you by the school and those items listed on your supply list inventory. Also, remember to get textbooks. Most of the textbooks are located in a securely locked area and must be issued to you by a member of the office personnel or other designated person. It is *extremely* important to maintain focus when completing these tasks.

Sometimes, the surfaces of the furniture will need to be washed. Ask the custodial staff to dust the furniture for you. If you have young, industrious children, relatives or friends bring them along to assist you in arranging the furniture into the floor plan design that you sketched previously. Next, have them to place student textbooks and other materials on or inside each desk or on tables. Direct them to put the remaining books in the bookcase or wherever you so designate.

Next, hang the background paper, borders, letters, pictures and other items necessary to complete all bulletin boards and wall hangings. This step will be relatively quick and easy since you have decided on and made in advance, the materials necessary to complete the displays for each board and wall hanging.

The furniture is cleaned and arranged, the textbooks and other items are on top or under the student's desks, the storage cabinets are unpacked and the bulletin boards and wall hangings are hung. It is now time to put the finishing touches on the classroom set up. Continue by stocking your teacher desk with office supplies and other items that you will use frequently. Place files folders, manuals, supplemental and resource materials, etc., into the file cabinet. Don't forget to, return all unused materials to the storage area, then clean all paper and scrap materials from the floor and work area. The physical classroom set up is now complete, except for special items and equipment that you need to borrow from the Media Center, Physical Education, Music and Art Teachers. It is now time to venture out of the classroom. Remember it is of the utmost importance that you maintain focus when venturing out of your classroom.

For special books, audio and media equipment, go to the Media Center (Library). First, find a rolling cart to use in transporting the AV materials to your classroom. These carts are usually located in or near the Media Center. Then, check out A.V. equipment such as a television, computer equipment and software, a cassette tape recorder, CD player and pre-recorded tapes, a record player and records, charts, maps, filmstrip projector and filmstrips, and games. Please be conscious of the time limit placed on returning the materials, so that other teachers can borrow them. If you need to extend the time limit on a certain item to complete a lesson, get clearance from the Librarian first, to make sure that no one is on the reservation list for that particular item. If another teacher is on the waiting list for that item, you can always check them out at a later date.

Visit the Physical Education Teacher to check out P.E. equipment for the days that your class does not have P.E. and recreation equipment for those "bad weather" days when you have to stay indoors. Invest in or use your school budget to buy games such as Simon, Perfection, Backgammon, Checkers, Boggle, Scrabble, Candy Land or other board games and table top or floor recreation equipment. Be sure to place a sign-up sheet in each box to reduce the confusion of who is next in line to play the game. Ask the Art Teacher for special supplies and the Music Teacher for musical instruments and equipment. Immediately place each item in a designated place. When touring your classroom on the first few days of school, explain to your students the importance of replacing this equipment in the proper places.

Store all boxes. Flatten the boxes if possible, because boxes are hard to find during packing time at the end of the school year; it will also maximize storage space. Store papers, and other materials in the storage areas, as well. Your classroom should now look complete. You should be proud of your accomplishment to this point because you have covered a lot of ground. You are now ready to receive visiting parents and students.

DIAMOND CHECKPOINTS

The following setup outline will help you during this most crucial time. Refer back to this outline as often as possible.

- Make sure furniture is clean and dusted
- Arrange desk, center tables, chairs, and bookcases
- Place textbooks on student desks
- Hang bulletin boards and other wall hangings
- Set up discipline model and helpers charts
- Set up interest centers
- Unpack boxes and cabinets
- Stock teacher desk and file cabinet
- Check A.V. equipment, books, tapes, etc., from the Media Center
- Check our P.E., music and art supplies and equipment
- Flatten and store empty boxes

"An organized beginning will set the pace for the remainder of the year."

CHAPTER 3
"SCHOOL MUSTS"
THE BEGINNING

OBJECTIVES

- To inform teachers of some of the procedures involved in starting a school year.
- To help them organizes the task into simple, workable steps.

MOTIVATION

- To help guide teachers through one of the busiest times of the school, without feeling overwhelmed by the amount of work involved in creating a successful classroom system.

The first day of school is the busiest day of the school year. Let's take a look at some of the first day of school *musts*. If you have not already been told, you will wear many hats, because teaching is the most diverse profession of all times, and has been that way since the beginning. You are a leader, counselor, secretary, clerk, mediator, coach, a debate team leader, organizer, promoter and a nurse, just to name a few.

When you arrive, for the first day of school, check with the central office for your final student roster. Check to see if there have been any changes in your roster so that you can update your roster or make adjustments to your pre-printed nametags.

Greet students and parents at the door. Check their name off the list as they enter the room. For the first week or two, most school systems require each teacher to take a class count. A class count consists of the number of boys and girls of each ethnicity that is in attendance in your class. This count is to be sent to the central office by a certain time each morning.

Explain the daily routine to the students placing emphasis on what they are expected to do when they arrive in the morning. Also, discuss what steps to take in preparing for lunch and dismissal in the afternoon. Because lunch is a time for a mental break and nourishment, students tend to get overly anxious about it. It is a time when they will get a chance to see and possibly visit with their friends from another classroom.

Reviewing class rules, behaviors and consequences on the first day of school is extremely important. It sets the pace for the remainder of the school year. *NOTE*: Some consequences will need second and third offense standards, with the third being a trip to the assistant principal's office for further actions to be taken outside of the classroom. Make a chart or board listing these rules and consequences and display it in the classroom. Make a hard copy for your files with each student's signature of agreement.

Discuss lunchroom and hallway behavior. Let the students know what you expect and the consequences that stand behind each violation. In establishing the rules, involve the students in creating the consequences, using the democratic method. For example, your lunch procedure may go like this: At the signal to stop all work, students are to clean their work area, wash their hands and proceed to get their lunches, lunch money, or lunch cards. Next, they are to form a line at the exit door to the classroom according to the method of lunch they will be receiving; those who have free or reduced lunch cards line up first, those who are buying lunch next and those who brought lunch from home last. At the conclusion of the lunch period, those students chosen as cafeteria helpers remove their trash first. They then proceed to clear the tables of any remaining debris left by the class. The other members of the class after clearing the area where they ate, proceed to the trash bins, then line up at the exit door of the cafeteria. If you so choose, a fifteen-minute recess will give students of any grade level an added release period, followed by a restroom break. Then it is back to work. You may even choose to delay this recess period for later in the day, when students may seem to get restless.

Always have walk-through fire and disaster drills during the first week, so that your students will know where to go and what to do in case of an emergency. You should find this information in your School Handbook for Teachers. Post a fire escape route near the exit door of your classroom, as well as in the Substitute Teacher Handbook. This handbook is assembled by you and is inserted into a folder or binder. It contains information that your substitute teacher should know about your students and classroom procedure when you are absent from school. Include such information as your daily schedule, seating charts, lunch schedule, class rules and consequences, special instructions, classroom helper chart and its rotation, specialty classes (P. E., Art, Music and Library etc.), reading and math groups.

Assign all books and supplies on the first day of school, so that the students will develop an urgency for learning. By this time the books should already be on the students' desk. Discuss the importance of keeping up with and being responsible for their textbooks. Also, share with them the replacement cost for each book should it be lost or damaged in any way.

Discuss Interest Centers in the first week of school. Start with one center at a time and explain the procedure for using each. For example, have the students sign into each center (so that you can monitor the flow and completion of each assignment). Have at least three different activities, including a manipulative (hands on) assignment, a challenge (for creative thinking) and a writing activity (to evaluate their understanding of the concept explored).

It is always a good idea to use classroom helpers to give students duties to challenge their memory, creativity and responsibility levels. Duties such as conducting opening exercises, sharpening pencils, office runner, attendance clerk, lunchroom monitors, teacher's assistant or a host of other duties can make up an array of challenges for students on a rotating scale. You will decide how to rotate names to reduce the stress of students saying, "I have not had a turn." Determine the rule for student name rotation, daily, bi-weekly or weekly.

The first day and week of school are the busiest and most exciting times of the school year. If planned and organized well, you will have a virtually stress-free and a controlled start for many school years to come. Remember, "Practice makes perfection easier."

DIAMOND CHECKPOINTS

The following "School Musts" outline will assist you during the first day and week of school.

- Confirm final student roster with the main office
- Greet students and parents at the door
- Turn in class count and attendance on or before the designated time
- Introduce, discuss and have students sign and date the Class Rules Agreement
- Explain the concept of a fire drill practice and do a walk-through
- Discuss hallway and lunchroom procedures
- Discuss the daily routine
- Assign books, supplies and other materials
- Introduce and discuss Interest Centers
- Introduce and discuss Class Helpers and Duties

"The key to good record keeping is recording data into pre-determined places."

CHAPTER 4
RECORD KEEPING

OBJECTIVES

- To identify vital records.
- To organize state and school system records.
- To organize class records and folders.

MOTIVATION

- To organize the clerical system for ease of accessibility and maintenance.
- To be able to records locate record, data and materials with ease of accessibility.
- To eliminate the hassle of searching for needed files without taking away from instructional or planning times.

One might say that education is a system that is saturated with record keeping. If this is the case, it is only a reflection of the systems in the world in which we live. One of the concerns of teachers is, "Will we have a teacher assistant this year?" Some kindergarten and special needs teachers have full-time teacher assistants, first and second-grade teachers might have half-day assistants, third through six grade teachers might have a teacher assistant possibly two hours per day. However, these assistants are not allowed, by law, to be responsible for keeping teacher records current. For example, if there is a discrepancy in your attendance records, the teacher is held responsible and must show proof and explain the error to the proper school officials.

Unfortunately, there are not many school systems that give clerical help to teachers; therefore, it is up to the teacher to know what is expected of them. As educators, we know that recording information is extremely important to building and maintaining a good record keeping system that will be helpful and reduce paperwork stress. In some cases, it is the means by which we get paid. Recording data can be easier to manage if the system is organized from the beginning. Let's take a look at the different aspects of record keeping:

Permanent Record Folders: The first step is to secure a class list and pull the permanent record (PR) folders from the school vault. Check the folders out through the main office or the counselor's office. Make a class information sheet, see *CS Form A*. You can find this and other reproducible copies listed in the Resource List at the end of this book or you may obtain copies of the Classroom Secrets Every Teacher Must Know (New *Teacher 101*) *Resource Package* on the website. From the PR folders, record student names, addresses, home telephone numbers (use a pencil when recording the addresses and telephone numbers, because they sometimes change during the school year). Also include birth dates, social security numbers, beginning reading, math and language arts levels, parent or guardian names and work telephone numbers. This information will prove to be very helpful throughout the school year, because you will have student information at your fingertips when completing forms, calling parents, formulating groups and organizing different activities. If you are fortunate enough to have a teacher assistant, this would be an excellent job for her or him to undertake. Always remember to return the PR folders to the school vault after each use, it's the law.

Student Class Folders: Create two folders for each student. One for collecting class work and the second one is a confidential conference folder. When filing these folders, use dividers and label one section "Work Folders" and the other section "Confidential Folders." This is another good job for your teacher assistant or parent volunteer.

Textbook Records: On the first day of school, record all of the student textbook numbers, so that there will be no confusion, and you will have these numbers in case their books are lost. If your school system does not have a form, you may refer to the Resource List *CS Form B* or reproduce it from the resource package. Alternate pen and pencil colors so that it will be easily read when referring back to the list. To save time have student textbooks already on their desks. You can make book distribution and record book numbers a part of the first day or week of school activities. Or to save time, have students' textbooks on their desks when they enter the classroom on the first day of school.

The Roll Book: Read the directions carefully and follow the specific instructions given by your school system. Each school system has different ways in which they want information to be recorded. Some school systems require teachers to keep attendance and test scores in their roll book, while another system might require a daily attendance record and all grades, whether they are tests or class work. Some systems do not require any specific marks be kept in the roll book; rather they leave it to the discretion of the teacher. Be sure to ask questions.

Attendance Records: A school record of student attendance can be a legal document, just as a roll book can be a legal document if a court subpoena is issued. Consequently, most of the educational dollars are centered on student attendance, as well as teacher paychecks. Some school systems use the average daily attendance of students, and some use the number of bodies in the classroom to determine how the educational dollars will be spent. In some states, the amount of teachers' pay raises and the number of teachers hired are also given consideration when dealing with student attendance ratios. The mark that you make in your roll book and on the attendance registrar translates into chalk, books, paper, maps and your paycheck.

For example, if John has a consistent pattern of being tardy to school, then one day is caught shoplifting at a nearby convenience store, and you accidentally mark him present, you will find it difficult to explain to your principal, the storekeeper and law officials, the discrepancy in your record keeping system. Make sure of your accuracy when recording attendance data, especially if your school system uses the computer attendance method.

Classroom Attendance: In middle school, high school and other schools where students go to more than one class per day, teachers are usually required to take attendance. Do remember to take attendance because some students may skip class and the teacher is responsible for reporting in-school absentees. Do not depend on the homeroom absentee list, because it may not include late comers. Remember that it is important to keep accurate attendance records because student attendance is the life of school systems.

The Lesson Plan Book: Some roll books are equipped with a lesson plan section; find out if this is the official lesson plan book or if you must create one. Your supervisor may have a lesson plan format for teachers to follow. Make sure that you know which one to use and what information is required to be in all lesson plans. This information may include curriculum objective numbers, Teacher Edition pages or student book page numbers, materials needed to teach the lesson or the number of assignments required to complete the lesson. Optimize the amount of information that is readily available to you at a glance. It will be helpful to you when making transitions between lessons. There is more on lesson planning in a later chapter.

Standardized Test Records: Some states, school systems, charter and private schools are allowed to choose whether standardized tests are administered as a part of their academic curriculum. The record of each student's test results is an excellent indicator of their levels of strengths and weaknesses. These records can be used to develop an individual academic action plan for each student's academic growth and achievement. More on testing in a later chapter.

Academic Chart: Developing an academic chart at a glance can be very useful in keeping abreast of student work-study habits and how well students understand concepts taught. It also provides a vehicle for monitoring which students need more help, who needs more advanced work or it may reveal that you may need to take a different approach to teaching a specific lesson, in any area of study. Refer to the list in Resource List, *CS Form C* or reproduce it from the resource package. This list has a two-fold purpose: (1.) to chart each student's overall progress and (2.) to chart the progress of all students in any subject area. This chart is not intended to replace the teacher grade book, only to assist in charting the progress of your students.

Materials Record: Keep a folder with a list of materials that you borrow from the library, P.E. art, music departments, teachers and other school personnel. Also, keep a list of materials and equipment that others borrow from you. A lot of valuable personal materials can be lost during your years as an educator, if you do not have your colleague list, sign and date a release form of items borrowed from you. Just think about it, you will know who to go to and retrieve your articles when you need them.

Meeting and Memo Records: Create file folders for (1) all faculty meeting agendas and other meetings, (2) notes from the principal's and main office, (3) district or school system memos and notes to and from parents. It is far better for you to have this information organized than to search frantically for papers that you need in a hurry, to complete an urgent report or to meet a deadline. Place all information compiled into you file cabinet or desk for easy access.

When records are organized, recorded properly and updated regularly, the clerical part of being an educator is not overwhelming. By law each teacher is to have a daily planning period, by scheduling this time wisely, you can achieve a maximum organized reporting system. Good record keeping helps to relieve paperwork stress. In the next chapter, let's take a look at reporting information that has been compiled, such as report cards, grade level and school system reporting.

DIAMOND CHECKPOINTS

The following is a list of the different types of records that a teacher is responsible for maintaining throughout the school year:

- Permanent Record Folders
- Student Class Folders
- Textbook Records
- The Roll Book
- Attendance Records
- Classroom Attendance
- The Lesson Plan Book
- Academic Charts
- Standardized Test Records
- Academic Records
- Materials Records
- Meeting and Memo Records

"Collecting and reporting data is one of the main thrusts in education."

CHAPTER 5
REPORTS

OBJECTIVES

- To familiarize teachers with the different types of reports used in educating children.
- To give a brief synopsis of these reports.

MOTIVATION

- To help teachers understand that there are many reports that are required to be completed to show accountability for student achievement.
- To help teachers understand that being held accountable for various reports is very much a part of the education system. Returning them with accuracy and efficiency is a plus when it comes to evaluations given by your supervisor.

In the field of education, a lot of paperwork is done in the form of reports. There are reports and questionnaires given to you by the school system, the school administration, the grade level, student reports, progress reports, reports to parents, report cards and weekly reports. If you are a special education teacher, there are IEP's (Individual Educational Plans), forms of documentation, daily progress forms, forms to fill in for specialists who work with your students, ARD/IEP meeting forms, diagnostician request forms, evaluations forms and other reports, just to name a few. The main thing to remember is, the more information that is compiled ahead of time, the fewer headaches you will have in gathering the information when it is needed. Let's take a look at the main ones.

Grade Level Reports are mainly for charting the progress of the students on your grade level as a whole. It reveals the number of students on a certain level in a specific subject. One of the main reasons for this type of charting is preparedness for standardized testing.

Weekly Reports can be sent home to parents along with their work to inform them of their child's academic levels as well as a student's social, school and classroom behavior. Remember to include words of praise for even the smallest achievements and ideas and suggestions on improving academic and/or social behaviors. This can be done through handwritten notes, pre-printed checklists or by creating you own form. In some school systems this step is optional and in others it is mandatory.

Progress Reports are usually sent home midway through a semester or quarter, to inform parents of their child's current progress. At this point, a parent/teacher conference can be set to discuss strategies to improve a student's academic and/or social behaviors. At the beginning of the school year, your teacher assistant or school volunteer can fill in the top portion of the reports with students' names, teacher's name, grade level, and other identifying information, to save time when completing these reports. NOTE: Please check the information recorded on these and any other reports written or entered into a computer by others, because in the end, you are ultimately responsible.

When the reports are returned, check to make sure they are signed and dated. It may be a requirement that you place these progress reports in the student's PR Folders. If this is the case, file them when you have received all or most of them (some reports will take longer to come back than others). If this is not a requirement, file them in each student's conference folder for future reference.

Report Cards are sent home at various times, depending on the reporting period of each school system. Some have nine-week reporting periods, some have six-week reporting periods and in the case of private schools, these periods may be longer. In any case, be prepared. If you teach a primary grade, make a report card holder for each student's report card. It can be made with folded construction paper and laminated, if possible, for reuse over the course of the school year. When the report cards are returned, check off the student's name, so that you will know which ones have not yet been returned. At this point, reminders can be sent home to expedite the return of the remaining report cards. Believe me, there will always be times when the report card will be eaten by the family dog or mangled by a baby brother or sister. Make sure they are signed and dated. In some school systems report cards are to be kept in the student PR Folder (Personal Records Folder) at all times. Check with your school to determine what is required. In some school systems, the last report card is sent home via the US Postal Service. Check with your school to find out if each student is responsible for supplying a self-addressed stamped envelope for this purpose or if the school supplies this service. Some teachers even choose to do it themselves (it's a great tax write off!).

Routinely update the attendance and grade sections of the PR Folder when completing the report cards. It may be best for you to fill in this information yourself because, at the end of the school year, these numbers must add up to the total amount of days that school year was in progress. For example, if school is in session for 190 days, then student days present and days absent must equal 190 days at the end of the school year. Also, at the end of the school year, you are responsible for averaging and recording grades, recording reading, math and language arts levels, closing remarks, promotion and retention status, and recording levels of achievement and behavior levels.

Certificates and Awards are a part of the report card process. Students who have achieved high honors deserve to be awarded, just as students who have accomplished very little. The reason for this is children learn and acquire understanding at different degrees and levels. When completing report cards, list by category, students who have perfect attendance, honor roll students, principal's list students and other honor categories for Awards or Honors Day. This is a day set aside by the school to acknowledge students who have done exceptionally well in academics, attendance and other areas of recognition. Even those students who have not accomplished the higher honors deserve a certificate, given by you in front of the class, to help boost self-esteem and confidence, especially in elementary school. Give awards only if they really deserve it, not because they will be left out of the awards ceremonies. However, you have the final say on who deserves what kind of award based on their academic and behavioral performance.

Organizing your classroom management program will make it more successful, and it will alleviate last minute stresses. Formulate a consistent pattern of recording data. By organizing your daily planning period times, you can use part of this time each day to update information or all of this period on one or more days during the week to record data into your system.

In the next chapter, we will find out why schedules are important to your academic program, to the school syste and in maintaining control in the classroom.

DIAMOND CHECKPOINTS

Listed below are some of the reports that will need your attention.
- Grade Level Reports
- Weekly Reports
- Progress Reports
- Report Cards
- Certificates and Awards

"Schedules are formats that are not etched in stone."

CHAPTER 6
SCHEDULES

OBJECTIVES

- To understand the importance of schedules.
- To set up different types of schedules.

MOTIVATION

- Following a plan of action is much easier than chasing the wind. Students learn more progressively when organized teaching takes place.

Consistency is a major key to learning. Setting and following schedules routinely will assist in the learning process. To maximize the productivity in the classroom, develop a working schedule or routine that is tailored to fit your teaching style. Keep in mind that scheduling school holidays and programs will always deviate from the regular class schedule. Visualization can play a significant part in setting up the class routine. Sit back and let your mind roam free and then ask the question, "How do I want my program to flow from the beginning to the end of the day?" Then picture in your mind each part of your day.

Let's envision the first part of the day from 7:30 AM - 8:30 AM in the morning. During this time, you will greet the students as they arrive. This is a vital information gathering time, where you will find out how each student feels physically, mentally and emotionally. Briefly, but genuinely listen to their stories as they enter. From 7:30 AM - 7:50 AM, the students will remove their homework from their bags and put it in the designated place. Next, they will place silent reading books, papers and pencils on the desk, after which, they will proceed to the free center areas to play games. If they have not finished their homework or other assignments, this would be an excellent time to do so. At 7:50 AM, give the signal for clean-up time, after which the students will proceed to their seats to begin the day. From 8:00 AM - 8:10 AM is opening exercises. This includes the Pledge of Allegiance, a patriotic song, silent meditation or prayer, roll call, the current event of the day and/or sharing. To ensure that each student has an opportunity to participate, create a list. Next, change the names on the Helper Board (it would be wise to develop a system for rotating the names). Continue to visualize each part of your day, and new creative ideas will come. It would be wise to create a weekly and yearly calendar of events including holiday events and celebrations, birthdays, field trips and school programs. Do not forget to record your thoughts on paper or they might be lost forever!

When developing your schedule and routine, consider the following components:

- The beginning of the school day activities such as free center time, homework completion period, sharpening pencils, etc.

- Opening exercises, such as the pledge, a patriotic song, silent meditation, reciting positive affirmations, roll call, current events, student helper chart, etc.

- Silent reading, journals, sharing with a partner etc. Take advantage of this time by completing reports that must be sent to the office, attendance reports and lunch count tabulations, reviewing the daily schedule or the first lesson of the day.

- Time spent out of the classroom for restroom breaks, lunch and recess.

- The time spent in specialty classes such as art, music, P.E., computer lab, library, etc.

- The amount of time spent on teaching each subject area per day. Some school systems require a certain amount of time be spent on each subject area per day or per week.

The following is a sample copy of a daily schedule for an elementary school. Middle school and high school schedules can be adapted to include each period of the day in which you teach your subject area. A listing of this form can be found in Resource List, *CS Form D* or reproduced from the resource package.

SAMPLE DAILY SCHEDULE

Time	Minutes	Activity
7:30-7:50	20	Free Center Activities
7:50-8:00	10	Clean Up
8:00-8:15	15	Opening Exercises
8:15-8:30	15	Silent Reading, Journals
8:30-9:15	45	Language Arts (Reading)
9:15-9:25	10	Restroom Break
9:25-10:00	35	Math
10:00-10:30	30	Social Studies
10:30-11:15	45	P.E./Music/Art/Library
11:15-11:45	30	Science/Health
11:45-12:00	15	Clean Up; Prepare for Lunch
12:00-12:30	30	Lunch
12:30-12:45	15	Recess
12:45-1:15	30	Language Arts (Spelling)
1:15-1:45	30	Language Arts (Handwriting)
1:45-1:55	10	Restroom Break
1:55-2:15	20	Creative Writing
2:15-2:25	10	Clean Up/ End of The Day
2:25-2:30	5	Dismissal

Schedules will change according to daily activities. Setting up a weekly schedule will help you in planning future events, special projects, programs and selecting a day for parent conferences and other meetings. Parent conferences will be discussed in a subsequent chapter.

The Weekly Schedule is important when adjusting your normal routine. A listing of this chart can be found in Resource List, *CS Form E or* reproduced from the resource package. When filling in this chart, write the major subject areas in each block and then add to these subject blocks all specialty classes and other activities that deviate from the major subject areas.

Let's say for example, that your class needs to rehearse for the spring musical and this will continue for two weeks or so. Use the previous Daily Schedule as an outline. By looking at your weekly schedule, you find time to practice in the morning during your social studies block and in the afternoon as part of the language arts block. By using these times, you will still fulfill the state and school requirements for the number of minutes each day or hours per week spent in social studies and language arts.

There are states and school systems that require teachers to keep a working record of the number of minutes per day and/or week that each subject is taught. This is called Timeline Requirements. This means you are held accountable for the amount of time that you teach each major subject area. For example, let's assume that you must teach math a total of 175 minutes per week. In order to reach this goal, you would have to teach math a total of 35 minutes per day. To help you keep up with this scheduling, you might use *CS Form F,* which is in the Resource List. It can help you arrange and record your schedule.

Setting up your schedule will give you a working idea of how your days will run initially. Make changes as you go and grow. Be creative and sometimes ask your students how they want to spend or change existing free time. This will give you an idea of where their interests are. Have fun, but stay on task and you will have a rewarding year.

DIAMOND CHECKPOINTS

Listed below are calendars, events and activities that will assist you in organizing the pacing of your academic teaching schedule.

- Create a Yearly Calendar
- Monthly Calendar
- Weekly Calendar
- Daily Calendar
- Beginning of school
- Opening Activities
- Silent Reading Period
- Classroom Breaks
- Specialty Classes
- Time Spent on All Subject Areas

"Putting it all together is worth the time and effort."

CHAPTER 7
CURRICULUM INTEGRATION

OBJECTIVES

- To organize the curriculum.
- To compile all curriculum resources into one reference directory.

MOTIVATION

- To assist teachers in integrating the curriculum to meet the standards set forth by their state, school system, school and personal preferences.
- To strategically create a one-stop reference guide/manual for planning, preparing setting up lessons.

Curriculum Integration is a viable part of establishing a well-rounded school program. It will benefit teachers not only at the inception of a school year but year after year as long as the teacher remains in the teaching profession. Of course, if the teacher changes grade levels, the curriculum integration must be changed to accommodate the objective for that grade level.

Learning objectives for the school system, state, and textbook must be correlated in order to achieve the maximum learning potential of the students. Let's not forget the teacher's own personal and creative educational style. There is one other area that should be included in this integration process; the time associated with completing each objective as prescribed by the state or school system. The timeline is a monitoring tool to ensure that all objectives will be taught by the end of the school year.

By taking one step at a time, you will create a masterpiece of valuable information. You will have in your possession a quick and easy reference guide that will help you in planning lessons and writing lesson plans without doing the juggling act between books, manuals and written objectives. It will also aid in the preparation of each lesson with ease and efficiency.

The following steps will guide you through the curriculum integration setup. When completed, you will have at your fingertips a reference guide that will reduce time when setting up planning and preparing lessons.

Gather the textbook teacher's editions and the state and school system objectives. Choose a key objective instrument to begin the process. This instrument will be the main guide, where all other objectives will be added. Thoroughly review the objectives presented to you by the state, school system and textbooks. Decide which will be your key objective instrument. For example, let's use the school system objectives as the key objective instrument for math in kindergarten. Create a flow chart (See listing in the Resource List section, *CS Form G*) using the following headings: School Objective Number (School Obj. No.), School Objective (School Obj.), State Objective (State Obj.), Textbook (Textbk), Timeline (Time), Group Size (Group Lg/Sm) and Materials Needed (Materials). The following is a sample flow chart.

Math

Sch.Obj. No.	School Objective	State Obj.	Textbk.	Time	Group Lg/Sm	Materials
1.1	Count from 1-10	M-1	pp. 3-5	1 wk	lg.	None
1.2	Match and numbers from 1-5	M-4	pp. 6-12	2 wks	sm.	Number games, chips, number cards, counters

Be sure to make several copies of the original flow chart for continued use. You have several options in completing this chart, they are:

Complete one to ten objectives per subject area at a time. This means complete ten objectives in math, social studies, science etc. Then go back later and continue the process until all objective correlation are integrated.

Complete one unit at a time per subject area.

Complete one subject at a time. For example, finish the entire math curriculum before proceeding to the next subject.

Play it by ear and then record what you have done. Be really careful with this step, because it is easy to forget to record what you have done. Besides, it is more trouble than it is worth.

Insert the completed pages into a binder, with dividers for each subject area or in separate folders for each subject area. Store the Curriculum Integration Guide(s) in a place for quick reference after it is finished.

It would be a good idea to write lesson plans for the first two weeks of school and modify them as needed. Writing your lesson plans now will be a bonus, and you will be much more organized.

Sit back and relish the thought. You will not have to go through this process again next year or the year after that and so on and so on. For as long as you remain on the same grade level and the curriculum objectives do not change, this guide will be of extreme importance to you.

DIAMOND CHECKPOINTS

The following is a list of materials needed to create your curriculum guide for ease of lesson planning.

- Gather Textbook Teacher Editions
- State Standards Objectives
- School System Objectives
- Complete one unit at a time
- Complete one subject at a time
- Insert completed pages into a binder

"Teaching is the profession that teaches all other professions."

CHAPTER 8
TEACHING STYLES

OBJECTIVES

- To identify attributes linked to specific teaching orientations.
- To develop core principles and practices of classroom management.

MOTIVATION

As the new school year approaches, teachers busy themselves with planning lessons and organizing classrooms in anticipation of the new set of students. Unfortunately, one aspect is often omitted and in reflection may seem to be the most important teaching style. What kind of teacher are you? How does your ideal classroom look and function? What are your ideas concerning discipline and behavior management? All of these questions are keys to identifying the specific characteristics that are connected to the major teaching orientations: authoritative, behavioral and socio-emotional. There are benefits and shortfalls associated with each, but ultimately the individual teacher must explore his/her own perspectives about education, teaching and classroom management.

AUTHORITATIVE ORIENTATION

The authoritative teacher sets limits and guidelines for appropriate student behaviors in order to create an ideal classroom environment where learning can take place. In short, the orientation focuses on the teacher's responsibility to utilize different classroom management strategies to control behavior including rules, expectations, procedures, directives, mild desists cues, non-verbal cues and penalties. These practices work to increase productivity, organization, respect and efficiency among the students in the classroom.

The authoritative teacher assumes complete autonomy in the classroom but still allows the students a certain air of independence. They create and enforce all rules and expectations and conduct queries for the students' input. By explaining the basis for actions and decisions and allowing the class to contribute to the governing process, the discipline system is personalized, internalized and the students are more apt to adhere to the expectations. Rules, procedures and directives are all necessary for a successful and safe learning environment. In later chapters, you will find best practices for establishing a solid system of rules and procedures. Authoritative teachers are firm in their delivery but remain flexible to allow room for adaptability and modifications. The most important factor to remember is consistency.

BEHAVIORAL ORIENTATION

Educational theorist B. F. Skinner believed that behavior is learned and learning is influenced by events in the environment. Manipulating the environmental stimuli can change behavior. Children learn from consequences. They have learned to behave inappropriately and must learn appropriate behavior. Teachers who follow this school of thought achieve successful classroom management by utilizing tools of behavior modification including positive and negative reinforcement, logical consequences, self-monitoring and rewards. The overall aim of this approach to learning is to identify the source and reason for the behavior and implementing an appropriate intervention and to modify it when necessary. This supports a classroom environment conducive to learning.

Through positive (adding something) and negative (taking away something) reinforcement, the behavioral teacher seeks to invoke student behavior and attitudes that allow for the greatest occurrence of learning. Logical consequences provide an opportunity to teach students that they are ultimately responsible for the behaviors they choose. Often, teachers react and respond to the effect the behavior has on the learning situation instead of addressing the specific behavior. In this way, the student is made aware of the inappropriate behavior and receives consequences relating only to that behavior. The student gains an understanding of what he/she has done and will more likely choose the appropriate behavior in the future. A reward or token system presents the extrinsic motivation for achieving appropriate behaviors in the classroom. The promise of small prizes, classroom celebrations, extra center time or recess time are examples of incentives that can be used to reward students for engaging in desired behaviors.

SOCIO-EMOTIONAL ORIENTATION

Socio-emotional orientation describes teaching behaviors by which the teacher develops good interpersonal relationships and a positive classroom climate. Effective classroom management and effective instruction are largely a function of positive teacher-student and student-student interpersonal relationships where the teacher aims to connect with the students on a personal level. This approach is most effective when the teacher identifies the academic, social and cultural differences among the students and builds an understanding and respect for those differences. Students are engaged in a learning environment that appeals to their interests and encourage them to flourish "because of" not "in spite of."

The teacher must express genuineness when relating to the students and not be condescending. The teacher is guided by the fact that relevance and self-worth are part of the basic needs that these "small beings" require for feeling complete and purposeful. The teacher presents opportunities for student success through respect, recognition and responsibility. As the teacher connects with each student personally, he/she is building relationships that will increase productivity in the classroom.

REFLECTION

Effective teaching begins with identifying and understanding your personal teaching style. Although there are many other orientations associated with teaching styles, the three mentioned in this chapter are the most prevalent and prominent among educators. Some will find that there are combination teachers who display attributes of several different approaches. This is okay! The key is to find the system that works best for the teacher and the students with the ultimate goal of learning success.

DIAMOND CHECKPOINTS

The list below will assist you in determining which teaching style portraits your style of teaching.

- Authoritative Orientation
- Behavior Orientation
- Socio-Emotional Orientation

"How students learn is crucial to being an effective teaching."

CHAPTER 9
LEARNING STYLES

OBJECTIVES

- To identify the best way to teach each student.
- To identify the types of learning styles.
- To use identified learning styles to enhance student success.

MOTIVATION

- To familiarize teachers with the styles of learning.
- Knowing students learning style can increase their learning abilities.

What are learning styles? Learning styles are simply different ways of learning. It's the way students consistently respond to and use stimuli while learning. There are three basic ways that students grasp lessons being taught, through visual, auditory and kinesthetic/tactile learning. Some learners use a combination of these learning styles to fully understand lessons. Let's briefly explore each of these learning style:

VISUAL LEARNERS

Visual Learners need to see the teacher's facial expression and body language to fully understand lessons that are taught. They usually think in pictures and learn when videos, illustrated text books, overhead transparencies, flip charts, diagrams and hand-outs are being used. During classroom discussions, they take detailed notes and prefer to sit at the front of the classroom.

AUDITORY LEARNERS

Auditory Learners absorb information best *through listening*. They learn best by listening intensely to lessons being taught orally. They listen for the tone of voice, pitch, speed, by what others are using and other nuances to interpret the meaning of what is being taught. They benefit from reading aloud and using books on tape, CD/DVD, eBooks, music, etc. where the book content is read aloud.

KINESTHETIC/TACTILE LEARNERS

Kinesthetic/Tactile Learners are the movers, doers and touchy-feely type of learners. They learn best through the hands-on approach by exploring the physical world around them. They usually find it hard to sit still for long periods of time and may become distracted by their need for activity and exploration.

Identifying students learning style(s) is a way to maximize their learning capabilities. The teacher has several basic responsibilities and one of the most important steps in teaching students is first learning about and knowing how each individual student learns best. Once the teacher knows this information, he/she can plan and develop a variety of ways to address each student's learning style, understand what to expect from the mood, reaction and focus of each student while teaching. It is an excellent indicator for analyzing each student's understanding, and it's also an indicator on how to adjust and reinforce the concept that is being taught to encompass each student's ability to fully understand the content of the lesson.

When and how is this done? During the first week of school is the best time to administer a learning styles inventory because this is initial period of discovery, observation and information gathering about your students. It is also important to share the results with each student so that they will know and understand how they learn. In the future, they will be able to use this knowledge to self-direct their own learning and carry it into all phases of their learning environments and advanced levels of learning. Different learning style models can be found online, in bookstores or teacher supply stores. Always remember to secure the one that is appropriate for the age/grade level of your students.

DIAMOND CHECKPOINTS

The following is a quick reference tool to quickly identify the learning styles of learners.

- Visual Learners
- Auditory Learners
- Kinesthetic/Tactile Learners
- Use a Learning Style Inventory

"Where to start teaching is as simple as giving a test."

CHAPTER 10
TESTING

OBJECTIVES

- To define the basic responsibilities of teachers in the testing process.
- To define different types of tests.
- To identify testing styles.

MOTIVATION

- To familiarize teachers with the elements which are present in evaluating students.

Testing students is a means of measuring their knowledge of the objectives and lessons taught. In education, it is said that testing measures the teacher as well. It shows whether the student has learned the objectives that have been taught. When you are clear in your mind about the objectives you want students to learn, then the students will generally grasp the concepts being taught.

The teacher has several basic responsibilities before, during and after testing. Teachers must be sure:

Joycelyn Rhodes

- Students know how to take a test,
- The testing environment is planned carefully,
- The content area of the test is directly related to the objectives taught,
- To give the students a review for the test, and taught subject content,
- The students know what to expect from the teacher during the test,
- The directions are clear,
- To prepare students in case of an emergency, fire drill or disaster drill.

Teachers have a choice of using pre-printed tests or creating their own tests. When creating your own tests, there are six styles of test questions that should be considered. This allows for variety and it considers the fact that some students are better at certain types of test questions than others. Include the following styles of testing questions when creating your tests. Keep in mind the grade level that you teach; some styles of questioning may not be appropriate for all grade levels.

Multiple Choice questions give students a choice between three are four different answers. In turn, they will choose the response that best answers the question. Check with your school to find out if they have a Scantron test grading machine. This will be a time saver for you. If you are unfamiliar with this machine, it works like this; the students record their answers to the test on a Scantron sheet by filling in the circle next to the corresponding number choice with a No. 2 pencil. After the multiple-choice portion of the test is completed, the Scantron sheet is fed through the machine for grading.

Matching questions allows the student to choose the best response from Column A that matches the statement, word, or picture in Column B. In the primary grades, the students will do this by drawing lines between the columns that connect the right response. In the higher grades, they use numbers and letters to match the correct response.

True or False questioning is when a statement is made concerning the objectives, and the students enter T to represent the statement made is true and F to represent the statement made is false.

Fill in the Blank questions are a series of sentences that are written, whether in a paragraph or numbered sentence form, where a keyword has been omitted and a blank line replaces it.

Students are to select the best answer that completes the sentence. A list of these words are written either above or below the paragraph or sentences.

*Written Essay*s are a style of testing that gives the student one or more questions about the objectives taught. The students write brief essays about the questions. Specify in the directions whether grammar, spelling, sentence structure or capitalization will be a part of the grade. Pre-determine how you will allot points. Perhaps provide a rubric to better help the student structure their response and assess their performance.

Oral Tests are usually given on an individual basis. One or several questions are asked to determine whether the student understands the objective or lesson. Sometimes this test is given in a small group setting or in a large group as a review.

In the field of education, tests are administered for different reasons, but they are all designed to measure a student's abilities. There are employees hired (diagnosticians) to do specific testing for placement in different programs such as special education and advanced studies. However, in the classroom, the teacher is the diagnostician. The keys to successful testing practices are to develop your objectives clearly and keep your students comfortable with taking tests of various types, lengths and frequencies.

There are several ways in which you might have the students record their answers to tests. For example, you may have them write directly onto the test sheet, write on a separate, pre-formatted sheet provided by you, use a computer-generated sheet or use their own notebook paper. If you choose to use the test booklet from year to year, recording answers to the test on a separate sheet would be the best option. Also, a good point to remember concerning students writing on their own paper is to have them number their paper before they start the test to avoid confusion when recording answers. Let's take a look at the different types of tests.

Placement Tests are used to determine where students need to start their studies in any subject area. In kindergarten, students are given a pre-screening assessment. Keep in mind, some students may know more and some may know less than what the outcome of the test proves simply because of how they react to being tested and their level of maturity.

Pop Quizzes are usually a short review that is unannounced. It allows the teacher to find out if the students are grasping the objectives being taught. In some cases, it also assesses their study skills. The teacher will learn whether more teaching is needed in that subject area.

Objective Tests are given at the end of objectives studied. Like the pop quiz, it is a guide to determine whether the students should move to the next objective or for the teacher to re-teach the objective. If the majority of the class understands the objective, move on and assign peer tutors to those who need more help or have an after-school study group.

Weekly Tests keeps the students attuned to taking tests. It also monitors student 'short-term learning patterns. It prepares them for the unit test as well.

Unit Tests covers all of the objectives learned in the subject area. The length of the test is determined by the class time available or time allotted. This could range from 20 to 50 questions. You should include several sections with different learning styles. Use a standard answer key when grading this lengthy test.

Mid-term and Final Exams are one of the testing staples in the academic career of all students. Students begin to take these kinds of tests starting in the late elementary grades through high school. These tests usually carry a lot of weight when grades are being averaged. In some schools a special time is set aside for this purpose. If you choose to create your own test or if you are a part of a group involved in writing the questions for the test, remember these points. 1.) Choose questions from those that should have been learned. 2.) Write questions using several different styles. 3.) Go back and write clear and specific directions for each section. 4.) Assign points to each section that will total 100 points. 5.) Review the test and create a standard answer key for it.

All tests described previously prepare the students for standardized testing.

Standardized Tests measure the student's understanding of the subjects taught at their grade level. It is also compared with other students on their grade level in their school, school system, state and nationally. This test comes complete with student booklets, answer sheets and teacher instruction manuals. Study the manual carefully before administering the test to become familiar with the language and time limits of each section.

Overall, tests measure the students' ability to learn, understand and retain information taught. Developing your system of tests and measures now will be beneficial to you for years to come. Be creative, then label and save all tests for future use.

DIAMOND CHECKPOINTS

Listed below are the duties and responsibilities of both Teachers and Students during testing, as well as testing types and styles.

TEACHER RESPONSIBILITIES

- Make sure students know how to take tests
- Review for the test
- Make sure the content of the test is directly related to the objective taught
- Make sure that the directions are clear
- Make sure that the test environment is planned for carefully
- Be sure students know what is expected of you and them.
- Make sure they know the consequences for cheating
- Prepare them in case of emergency

BASIC TEST TAKING TIPS FOR STUDENTS

- Read directions carefully
- Start with question number one, continue through to the end
- Mark difficult questions, and then come back after completing all other questions
- Pace yourself
- Raise your hand to get the teacher's attention, if needed
- Review your answers before turning in your completed test
- If you finish before time is up, sit quietly

(cont.)

TESTING STYLES

- Multiple Choice
- Matching
- True or False
- Fill in the Blank
- Written Essay
- Oral Tests

TYPES OF TESTS

- Placement Tests
- Pop Quiz
- Objective Tests
- Weekly Tests
- Unit Tests
- Mid-term and Final Exams
- Standardized Tests

"Lesson planning is the key to organized learning."

CHAPTER 11
LESSON PLANS

OBJECTIVES

- To familiarize teachers with different types of lesson plan formats.
- To develop a comprehensive lesson plan.

MOTIVATION

- To help teachers understand the simplicity of lesson plan writing
- To show them what basic information that should be included in the lesson plan

Teachers have many different styles of lesson plan writing. There are those who are brief and to the point, others who include enough information to guide themselves, their supervisor or the substitute teacher to the lessons and materials. There are others who write long, detailed minute by minute lesson plans that even the non-professional can follow. Whichever style you choose, it is important to adhere to all regulations, because it might be a part of the teacher performance evaluation. Before setting up your system of lesson plan writing, ask your building supervisor about what information is expected to be a part of your lesson plans and ask what is the preferred form for classroom usage and submission for review.

The first two points to know and understand about lesson plans are: 1) There is no perfect lesson plan. 2) Lesson plans are written so that students can learn, not so that the teacher can teach what is expected of them. Once the basic concept of why lesson plans are written is understood by the teacher, then the question of where to begin follows.

At this point in the development of your management system, you have created a daily schedule, including state approved time recommendations, established the timeline for teaching each objective or unit and integrate the curriculum to include all available teaching resources. Now comes the questions of how to format the lesson plan, what components should be included, when to submit the lesson plan (daily, weekly, bi-weekly, monthly or by units of study) and where should the lesson plan be placed after completion. Let's address these questions so that you can establish your style of lesson plan writing.

Formatting First and foremost, find out if your school system or school supervisor has a set format and procedure for you to follow. If there is none available to you, then establish your own. Some teachers write long, detailed minute by minute lesson plans and others write simple notes to guide them through the lessons. In the Resource List *CS Form H 1-4,* you will find several formats including a lesson plan used in a unit of study in the resource package.

Lesson Plan Components In each lesson plan, include the objective number, explanation of the objective, daily activities, materials to be used and the evaluation.

Stating the objective number(s), in some cases, this enables you to meet the requirements of the state or school system in which you work. Also, it helps you keep track of those objectives that students have already learned and to keep abreast of those lessons that need to be taught.

Complete Objective Written Out This allows you to stay focused and on task. It allows anyone who comes into your classroom to observe or evaluate you and gives them the opportunity to look at your lesson plans to understand the content of the lesson you are teaching without having to interrupt you.

*Material*s The materials that you use may vary from day to day. Listing these materials on your lesson plans will save you the trouble of trying to locate materials at the last minute.

Planning ahead for materials enable you to research all available resources to enhance the learning objective and make it fun and informative for the students. Some materials may include textbooks and other books, audio and video tapes, charts, maps globes, games, manipulative, lab equipment, computer programs and software, films, special television programs, worksheets, workbooks and journals to name a few possibilities.

Evaluation The evaluation can be administered at different times during the objective learning process. However, *it is* important to note when you will check for student understanding of the objectives. This can be done by the students completing a worksheet, a pop quiz, or a formal, written or oral test at the end of the objective. The same procedure can be used if you develop a unit plan.

Comments The comments section can be added to any part of the lesson plan. If you choose a lesson plan format that is landscaped (where the paper is turned sideways), this space can be placed to the right. If you choose a format that is portrait (used the up-right position) the comment section can be placed at the bottom of the objective or page.

Whichever format you choose, the content of the plan is most important to your productivity. Write as much helpful information into your lesson plan as possible. Wordiness only takes up valuable space and accomplishes nothing, even though it may look good.

DIAMOND CHECKPOINTS

The following is a list of the different parts of a lesson plan.

- Formatting
- Lesson Plan Components
- The Materials
- The Evaluation
- The Comments

"Sharing with others means caring."

CHAPTER 12
OPEN HOUSE

OBJECTIVES
- To help teachers organize and set up for the event.

MOTIVATION
- To help teachers understand why Open House is a part of the school year.

Open House usually occurs in late September or early October. Parents, teachers, and students come together and explore the classroom environment. The parents are able to meet the teachers and other staff members, tour the school to see the changes that have taken place and join the PTA/PTO (Parent Teacher Association/Organization or other parent support organizations). They are able to examine the textbooks, review the curriculum objectives, learn about the teacher expectations and preview their children's class work and sign up for individual conferences. They are also able to learn about the specialty classes, find out about special programs, holiday celebrations and extracurricular activities.

In preparing for this event, you may choose to have a brief parent group overview (about ten to fifteen minutes in length) to share the issues listed above. It helps to answer some of the general questions parents may have in a small group rather than individually on that evening. If you choose this route, send memos home stating the place and time of the meeting; list the topics that will be addressed. Stress promptness, because some parents have more than one child enrolled and they will need to visit other classrooms.

To prepare for this introduction, write an outline of the issues to be shared. Allow a little time at the end of this session for other concerns that the parents may have. Be brief and point out areas that you would like for them to tour before they leave the room. For those parents that come in late or miss the overview meeting, politely, but firmly express that you will go over this information again at the individual parent conferences, then direct them to the Parent Conference sign up sheet. Do not be excessively concerned about being rude or insensitive. Like any other business, we as teachers work on a time schedule as well and we must abide by the rules that we set for others and ourselves.

To organize the classroom for the event, set up a table to display textbooks. A hint to the wise: do not display teacher edition books because they sometimes have a way of walking out of the door. Also include in this area, a list of materials and supplies that the students will need in addition to those supplied by the school. Place a sign in front of these copied sheets or copies labeled "Take One."

At the entry door, place two sheets of paper backed with different color construction paper, labeled "Sign in Sheet" for the attendance record of those who participated in Open House. This form can be found in Resource List *CS Form I*. Some schools give incentives to the class that have the most parents in attendance at Open House and other PTA meetings. Label the other sheet "Parent Conferences," this form is found in Resource List *CS Form J*. It gives the parent the opportunity to pre-register for parent conferences, to be held on a specific Parent Conference Day. This day has been pre-determined by your school administration before school started. I will provide more information on parent conferences later. If there are papers to be given out (normally called hand-outs) from your school or school system, staple the sets together and position them next to the sign in sheet and parent conference sheets. Make a sign that reads, "Important, Take One."

Place each student's sample work on the desk or table, have each student's name on the front page or in a manila folder in bold print. Be sure to tell the parents not to take the work home. You may choose to have some student work displayed on the bulletin board inside the classroom or on the wall outside of the classroom. Two points of caution; (1) be sure to display all students' work in one subject or another because you can easily damage the delicate self-esteem of the student's work that is not displayed; (2) check with the school administration about hanging work on the walls outside of the classroom because it may be in violation of a fire code or ordinance.

Keep your conversations with each parent brief that evening, even if they ask the classic question, "How is Johnny doing in class?" Give them a general, one-sentence overview of his progress. Then, *immediately* state that you will go into more detail at the parent conference because you have notes specifically written to share with them. Conversations should be very caring, but brief on this evening, simply because you must greet and chat with all who attend. Ask if they have signed up for a conference. Ensure them that the conference will enlighten them, and working as parent and teacher together we will work on their child's strengths as well as their weaknesses.

There will probably be a few parents still remaining at the conclusion of the Open House, however, begin to re-organize the classroom for the student's arrival the next morning. If you feel uncomfortable about doing this, say this, "Please excuse me, I *must* prepare for the boys and girls arrival in the morning." Continue to remove the students' folders from their desk or table. Collect the textbooks that were on display. Collect the sign in sheet (be ready to send it to the office in the morning) and the Parent Conference sign up sheet. Collect the material and supply list and all other papers and equipment that were used that evening. Move swiftly, because some parents will follow you around as you work; they should appreciate your efforts.

When your classroom reconstruction is finished, politely get your purse or other items; take out the keys as you head towards the classroom door. Thank them for coming out to support their child's efforts and for supporting the PTA. Ensure them that working as a team will give their child the best opportunity for reaching their full potential. Bid them a good night at the door to the classroom. If they continue to linger, walk with them to the school-building exit and say goodbye and that you will talk with them again at the parent conference.

Parents should leave the Open House meeting with more of an understanding of your objectives and expectations for their children. The teacher should leave with a sense of accomplishment in sharing one's self and the goals for the present school year.

DIAMOND CHECKPOINTS

This list will be extremely helpful when setting up for the beginning of the school year open house.

PARENT GROUP OVERVIEW

- Send home a memo announcing the event, stress promptness
- Write a brief outline
- Time limit; ten to fifteen minutes
- Briefly, review curriculum
- Preview teacher expectations
- View student sample work
- Learn about specialty classes
- Learn about special programs, holiday celebrations
- Learn about field trips
- Learn about extracurricular activities
- Set up Sign In Sheet
- Parent Sign up Sheet
- School and School system hand-outs
- Display sample student work
- Materials and supply lists
- Prepare bulletin boards
- Keep parent conversations brief

"Talking with parents is the best way to understand the student."

CHAPTER 13
PARENT CONFERENCES

OBJECTIVE

- To familiarize teachers with the procedure to follow when organizing parent conferences.
- To help them establish some parent conference rules.

MOTIVATION

- To help teachers understand that parent conferences are special times to learn more about their students through their parents. It also lets the teacher know more about the kind of support to expect from each parent.

Parent Conferences are the link between the parents, the teacher and the student. It gives more insight into the student's personality, behavior and character. It helps the teacher to find approaches to change, improve and enhance learning styles and social behaviors. It is also an indicator of how supportive the parent(s) or guardian(s) will be. The Parent/Teacher Conference Day usually takes place during the school day when the students are not in attendance. Prior to this day, try to get as many parents signed up as possible. Your first attempt to encourage parent participation was at the Open House meeting. Send home a notice of the date and times. In the letter, stress the importance of the meeting and include an employer appeal statement. As an option, you can add a section with questions for parents to think about, before attending the conference. Be sure to briefly address these questions during the conference and take notes. Ask questions such as: Does your child help around the house? What are his/her interest/hobbies? Does he/she have a regular study time? Does he/she wear glasses or contact lens? What is his/her attitude towards life? Also include a section on vital information update and a conference reply section.

    A sample letter can be found in Resource List *CS Form K*. Attach a copy of the conference schedule Resource *CS Form J* or copy it on the back of the letter to save paper. Show the times that are no longer available; to do this, write *Unavailable*, then write the first students names, next to the times already taken by conferences. Include your lunch and planning times. Send the letter home with all students one week before the conference date. You may simply choose to assign conference times. For those parents who have pre-registered, this will be a reminder and final confirmation. Do not be alarmed if the previously registered parents must reschedule. Give those who have not previously signed up first priority, then continue with those who return the confirmation slips immediately.

    Some conferences may need to be scheduled on a different day entirely. If this is the case, choose a designated parent conference day and time during your teacher planning period. Be sure to set the conference time towards the end of your planning period. This will give you time to set up for the next assignment or take care of any other business that you need to attend to before they arrive. Notify the main office of your expected arrivals when there are conferences beyond the designated planning day. You can do this the day before the conference or the morning when you get to work.

    Arrange your conference folders in the order of your conferences or if it is better for you, keep them in alphabetical order. Each conference folder should include, the bottom portion of the parent letter (the confirmation slip), a blank sheet of paper for taking notes, sample student work, and a parent contract.

    The Parent Contract is optional; a sample copy can be found in the Resource List CS Form L or reproduced from the resource package. It is a simple form that asks the parent to agree to help their child during this very special growth period in their lives. It asks that they help their child with homework, home projects, to talk with their child about academic, social and life issues. Also set aside time to discuss peer pressure, their emotional well-being, and to promote confidence and self-esteem building. The contract also asks that they spend at least five minutes each day listening to their child's cares and concerns. Be sure to have it signed and dated before they leave. If possible, give them a copy to take home or send a copy home at a later date.

Unfortunately, conference times are very limited. If time runs out before all issues have been discussed, make arrangements to continue the conference at a later date, if they so desire.

Thank them for coming and assure them that this school year will be among the best yet. Let them know that you look forward to working with them and achieving excellence with their child.

DIAMOND CHECKPOINTS

The following is list of steps to take when setting up parent conference schedules.

- Sign up as many parents as possible for conferences during Open House
- Send conference letters home one week before the conference day
- Send Parent Questionnaires along with conference letters (optional)
- Assign conference times (optional)
- Designate a parent conference day during one of your planning periods
- Arrange conference folders in the order of conferences, or alphabetical order
- Develop a Parent Contract (optional)

"Learning by doing is the best way to remember the lessons taught."

CHAPTER 14
SPECIAL PROJECTS

OBJECTIVES

- To identify different kinds of special projects.
- To help teachers understand that diversity is important to learning.

MOTIVATION

- To help teachers understand that deviating from the everyday studies is inevitable.
- Special projects with the proper planning and student involvement can be a rewarding learning experience for all.

Throughout the school year, there will be times when you will have to deviate from the regular class schedule. You will have to perform certain duties during programs, special events, field trips and celebrations. Good planning is a must in order to maintain peace in the midst of change.

Schoolwide Responsibilities In some schools, teachers have schoolwide responsibilities. The administration allows you the opportunity to choose from a number of committees, programs, duties and special events to be a member of or be the chairperson over. For example, let's say that you have the honor of being the chairperson over the American Red Cross Fundraiser.

This would mean that your responsibilities are scheduling committee meetings, advertising, setting and meeting deadlines, collecting and reporting the funds and a host of other duties that are involved in this campaign. This would mean that your loyalties are now divided between your Red Cross volunteer efforts and instructing your students. Even though this may be temporary, you still have to give it time and attention.

Grade Level Responsibilities The grade levels in your school may be held accountable for designing a bulletin board in the main lobby for a month, producing a play or decorating the school cafeteria for a certain holiday or observance. These are examples of more responsibilities in addition to your classroom and school-wide duties.

School Programs There may be annual school programs directed by the school music and physical education departments. These teachers use some or all of your students to participate in these programs. They also ask that the teacher assists in rehearsing the students when necessary. Some programs are sponsored by certain community groups who may come into the school and present information to students at different times during the year. These programs can range from an Arbor Day Celebration to a Drug Awareness Program.

Class Programs Class programs are required by some schools as a means of boosting confidence, self-esteem or as fulfilling a certain quota of programs for the school. This requires major decision making, planning, rehearsals, costumes, props, stage design and assisting students in learning their parts. It may seem overwhelming, but you will get through it, by coordinating school assignments with the work that you need to do for the program. For example, you will need a backdrop or pictures to decorate the stage for the performance. Use this time as part of your socials studies block (time) for several days until the project is complete. Class projects are also time consuming, but fun. Planning the steps that you need to take will help control the excitement of completing the project. An important point to remember is to involve all the students at all times whether they are working in one large group or divided into smaller groups.

Special Projects Special projects are a fun way to learn. Ask any child you know whether they are in elementary school, middle school (junior high) or high school. A special project in science might be to go outside and collect different kinds of leaves. Then, come into the classroom or go to the library and research and label the species found. These projects are a welcome break in the normal class routine. Some students are able to express themselves more creatively and absorb more information during this time.

DIAMOND CHECKPOINTS

The following is a list of "other duties as assigned" which could possibly be added to your primary responsibility of teaching your students.

- Establish the yearly theme or motto
- School-wide duties and responsibilities for teachers
- Grade level duties and responsibilities
- Programs and plays for students
- Class programs
- Class projects

"Field trips help the explorer experience reality."

CHAPTER 15
FIELD TRIPS

OBJECTIVES

- To learn how to pre-plan, organize and take a field trip.
- To learn how community resources are great learning experiences.

MOTIVATION

- To help teachers understand that field trips require a lot of planning. They are great hands-on learning experiences and good motivational tools for those students who do not have the opportunity to explore the community outside their neighborhood.

Field trips are a great way to learn and share outside the school environment. There is a lot of research and planning involved. Research your Policies and Procedures manuals within your school as well as for the school system in which you teach, (if you do not have a personal copy of the school system policies and procedures manual, you may go to the school library and check it out.

Consult with the grade level chairperson to find out if there are specific rules and procedures, beyond those policies that your principal prefers. Find out if the school system allocates funding for field trips. Find out about how many field trips you are allowed to take per school year. Also, determine if these trips can be taken as a class or whether they must be taken as a grade level. Ask if there is a specific procedure that you need to follow in applying for a field trip permit.

Field Trip Destinations After acquiring information concerning the policies and procedures of taking a field trip, select a field trip destination that is linked to your teaching units. Check with the facility to determine available dates, times, group sizes allowed at one time, and price per student and adult. If you teach handicapped students, check to make sure that the facility has the proper equipment to accommodate them. Choose a date and submit it to the school administration for approval. Once approved, send in a request for a bus(es) to the school system transportation department, this must be done at least two weeks prior to the field trip date.

Two weeks prior to the date of the field trip send home permission slips for parental approval, volunteer chaperones and ask for donations, if extra funds are needed. One week before the field trip send home a notice with instructions concerning the type of attire to be worn, lunch required and any other directives you deem necessary to ensure a successful venture. Make sure that each student has a name tag, for younger students and name cards for older students. Include the student's name, teacher's name, school name and telephone number. Make provisions for lunch. Your school cafeteria may supply lunches for those students who have qualified for free and reduced lunches by the state. Other students may buy their lunches from the school cafeteria at the regular price and still other students may bring their lunches from home. Whichever is the case, make sure that each student has a lunch during the field trip. Sometimes it may be better for the students to eat a good breakfast and wait until they return from a field trip to eat lunch. A mid-day snack can be provided for them to eat while on the excursion if you feel they might need to eat something.

Before boarding the bus or other modes of transportation, assign each student a "buddy" or partner. Explain to them that their "buddy" or partner will always be with them and if they need assistance, their buddy will go for help.

Review bus safety rules and proper school bus behavior. Have all students look at and become familiar with the people who are sitting on both sides of them, in front and in the back of them, because there will be a bus check done at the conclusion of the field trip. Also review personal behavior management while on the field trip and the consequences of unacceptable behavior while away from school.

Field trips are fun and exciting for both the students and teacher. They allow time away for the monotony of the school day and give students the opportunity to explore places they may never have seen or experienced before.

DIAMOND CHECKPOINTS

Listed below are some of the steps that will need your attention prior to the first days of school, at the beginning of school, right before and during the field trip.

- Acquire information concerning field trips at the beginning of the school year
- Find out the requirements and timelines for submission
- Request approval early because popular field trip destinations go quickly
- Make sure to give an assignment that relates to a course of study in the classroom
- Provide Name tags for all students
- Carry a field trip roster along with you
- Order lunches, snacks and drinks
- Take along a first aid kit

"When it's all been said and done, end it."

CHAPTER 16
"SCHOOL MUSTS"
THE END

OBJECTIVE
- To inform teachers of some procedures to follow when closing out the school year.

MOTIVATION
- To let teachers, know that the closing of school is the final busiest time of the school year and their rewards will not go unnoticed. It is also a good time to re-evaluate the school year and note any changes that would be preferred.

At the end of school, there is a reversal of some of the tasks accomplished at the beginning of the school year. Most school systems allot two to three days for teachers to complete records, store school materials and take home materials bought by you. This period of time usually begins after students are no longer in attendance. If you teach at a year-round school this cycle never really ends. You may want to refer back to Diamond Checkpoints in the chapter on "The Setup."

About two weeks or more before the close of school, set aside time to plan, organize and store away materials that you will no longer use. Below is a list of things you will need to accomplish in the last days of teacher planning:

- Unpack your desk and bookshelves.

- Return all AV (Audio-Video) and other equipment and materials that you have borrowed from the school.

- Remove all decorations, except bulletin boards (wait until the last day of school to remove these).

- Collect and store textbooks and reading materials (this is a good idea for locating lost books, before the last day of school).

- Collect materials that were borrowed from you by other teachers, so that they won't get packed away with their personal items or you may not see them again.

- Order materials you will need for the next school year. Most school systems allocate two hundred dollars per year for teachers to buy materials for their classrooms.

- Complete as much of the End of School Checkout List as possible before the end of the school year. Be sure to have the responsible person initial or sign it, because there will be a mad rush of teachers trying to beat the deadline at the last minute.

- Complete the reading and math records for you students.

- Complete the report cards, including the promotion and retention section. Exclude the attendance section until the last day of school. Remember the last report card is to be sent home through the mail, make sure that you have an envelope for each student; this will be handled differently in some school systems.

- Finalize the Permanent Record Folders. Include the final grades, average the grades, ending objectives in math, reading, and language arts, promotion and retention section, attendance and the total attendance for the school year, any special concerns, overall conduct grade, sign and date each.

- Box up sample student work, some schools require that you have sample work for the teachers to review for the next school year. Remember that you have kept this sample work in the student conference folders all year long.

- Make sure all students have turned in their library books or have paid the fine for lost books. Also, make sure that they have paid lunch charges.

- Make sure that each student has brought in a self-address, stamped envelope for mailing report cards home if this is a requirement for your school.

- Make sure that the desks, chairs, tables and bookcases are clear, clean and moved to the center of the floor. Classrooms are usually exterminated and the carpet is cleaned (if you are fortunate enough to have carpet) during the summer break.

- Have a final end of school conference with the principal or other school administrator.

- Make sure that your End of School Checklist has been initialed or signed by each person necessary. Remember your final paycheck depends on it.

Your journey is complete! You have reached a major milestone in your teaching career. You should feel more in control of your destiny because of your hard work and diligence. You have built a strong foundation that will continue to benefit you and your student for a life time.

DIAMOND CHECKPOINTS

The following list will be helpful in completing important data, records and forms, packing up, storing and returning materials and equipment at the end of the school year.

- Two weeks prior to end of the school year start packing away some items for summer break
- Unpack your desk
- Return AV equipment and books to the Library
- Remove decorations, keep bulletin boards up to the very end
- Collect and store books and reading materials
- Collect borrowed items
- Complete as much of the End of the Year Teacher Checkout Form before the last day of school
- Complete Math and Reading Records
- Complete report cards
- Finalize PR Folder information
- Enter Special Education student information
- Box up Sample Student Work
- Make sure students have returned all Library books, paid all fines and outstanding lunch fees
- Make sure each student has brought a self-addressed stamped envelope

- Make sure classroom furniture is moved to the center of the room
- Have an End of the Year Conference with your principal and/or immediate supervisor
- Make sure all items on your End of the Year Checkout Form is signed by the appropriate people.

"When counting to 10 is not enough, try a different method."

CHAPTER 17
STRESS MANAGEMENT

OBJECTIVES

- To help teachers handle stress when in the classroom.
- To help teachers de-stress themselves when on a break or whenever necessary.

MOTIVATION

- To help teachers to understand that stressful situations happen to everyone. But, how you react to the stress is the important issue to prepare for.

Today's teachers are under more stress and pressure than ever before. The Paperwork Reduction Act seems to bring about more paperwork. We must respect the religious rights of our students by omitting certain words from our vocabulary or possibly face a lawsuit. Some parents are more aggressive because they know they have certain rights, and they try to use them against the school for their own purposes. And of course, there may be peer jealousy within the school faculty. You must also stay on task with other teachers on your grade level as mandated by the educational government agencies. There is also the unspoken pressure of preparing students for national standardized testing right before spring break.

Moreover, students today seem to have more rights than teachers it seems and the majority of them know it. If you speak firmly to them, even touch them on the shoulder or give them a hug, you may face grave consequences. In some instances, it's your word against theirs.

In addition, the stresses of a teacher can come from many outside influences such as: students bringing troubles from their dysfunctional home life to school, discipline problems, low self-esteem, lack of confidence, disruptiveness, abuses, disobedience, insecurities, learning disabilities and Attention Deficit Disorder (ADD) and other disorders, which seems more prevalent in children today. Because so many parents must work outside the home, the lack of proper home training and sheer immaturity are among the character traits that teachers must address on a day-to-day basis. Also, teachers are expected to be on their feet moving for most of the hours that they're at work. Usually fatigue will set in before the end of the day. There is also the stress on the teacher's vocal chords.

So what do you do when you can't escape the stress during a grueling day? We'll take a look at some of those stress-busters, but first, let's take a brief look at how stress affects teachers and some warning signs.

Feeling "stressed-out" has psychological, emotional and physiological effects on our bodies that include the feelings of being trapped, backed into a corner, explosive emotional feelings inside, and being pushed to the limit. Feeling helpless, hopeless, anxious, perplexed, and confused are some of the effects that stress may cause. Some of these are easier to release than others, but be aware of the side effects that silently invade your being, mentally, physically and emotionally.

Look for the immediate warning signs of stress. Some might happen suddenly, and some may seem to build up over time. Headaches, fatigue, dizziness, feelings of weakness, neck, shoulder and back tension are some warning signs. Irregular heart rate, insomnia, nightmares, indigestion, constipation, impulsive behavior, irritability, inability to concentrate or focus your thoughts, excessive worry or loss of appetite or overeating. These are some of the symptoms that come along with stress. Become familiar with these signs and learn to apply the stress busters. The stress busters that follow will help you maintain the upper hand when situations try to get the best of you.

First, recognize that you are "stressed-out" or about to enter into a stressful situation. Then, take a minute to locate the area in your body that is being affected by the stress. Work with a technique to immediately release the tension and pressure, as soon as possible, even if it means separating yourself from your class or whatever situation that has triggered a stressful reaction.

Only a few procedures have been listed that have proven to be beneficial in dealing with anxiety within the teaching profession. By no means did we try to give you clinical methods or techniques for relieving stress. However, we urge you to contact your physician for stress-related symptoms that do not respond to simple, non-prescriptive techniques.

Good luck in your teaching career. You are a true humanitarian by simply choosing to teach our most valued resources – the students!

DIAMOND CHECKPOINTS

The following stress buster list is a quick reference tool that will be helpful during times of great need.

- Meditation
- Laughter
- Counting backward from 10
- Walking during lunch, planning period, during recess or
- after school
- Avoid school gossip
- Do absolutely nothing for five minutes
- Neck rolls
- Bend and stretch in standing or sitting position
- Ragdoll release (bend over from the waist down and let your arms dangle loosely)
- Recite positive affirmations
- Arm stretches - ballet curls
- Shoulder rolls
- Body twists
- Apologize when you're wrong
- Deal calmly and openly with those who upset you
- Gently and politely say "no" when asked to take on more projects

RESOURCE LIST

CS FORM A Class Information Sheet ....from page 16

CS FORM B Textbook Report ....from page 17

CS FORM C Academic Checklist ....from page 18

CS FORM D Daily Schedule ....from page 27

CS FORM E Weekly Schedule ....from page 28

CS FORM F Time Requirement Schedule ....from page 28

CS FORM G Objective Flow Chart..from page 32

CS FORM H-1 Weekly Lesson Plan ....from page 50

CS FORM H-2 Block Schedule Lesson Plan ....from page 50

CS FORM H-3 Individual Lesson Plan...from page 50

CS FORM H-4 Unit Plan..from page 50

CS FORM I Open House Sign In Sheet ....from page 54

CS FORM J Conference Schedule ....from page 54

CS FORM K Parent Conference ....from page 58

CS FORM L Parent Contract ....from page 58

BIBLIOGRAPHY

All the Things You Need to Know About Setting Up a Classroom. Dr. Lana Rosing, Ed.D. https://books.google.com/books?isbn=145001643X. 2010

An Easy Guide to Setting Up Your Grade K-5 Classroom. Article- https://www.scholastic.com/teachers/articles/teaching-content/easy-guide-setting-your-grade-k-5-classroom/

Bringing Out the Best in Teachers, What Effective Principals Do. Joseph Blase/Peggy C. Kirby. Corwin Press, Inc. New Berry Park, CA 91320. 1992

Classroom Management Guide for Substitute Teachers. Bonnie Moon. Outskirts Press, Inc. 2013

Classroom Organization: The Physical Environment. https://www.scholastic.com/teachers/articles/teaching-content/classroom-organization-physical-environment/

Classroom Setup and Organization Classroom. https://www.scholastic.com/teachers/collections/teaching-content/classroom-setup-and-organization/

How to Set up a Classroom for Students with Autism. Autism. Classroom.com. 2012

Index of Learning Styles Questionnaire Soloman, Barbara A, First Year College, NCSU. http://www.engr.ncsu.edu/learningstyles/ilsweb.html

Instructional Materials. Raymond V. Viman. Charles A. Jones Publishing Company, Worthington, Ohio. 1972

Kicking Your Stress Habits (A Do-It-Yourself Guide for Coping with Stress). Donald A. Tubesing. Whole Person Associates, Inc., Duluth, Minnesota. 2012

Learning to Teach...Not Just for Beginners: The Essential Guide for All Teachers. Linda Shalaway. Scholastic, Inc. 2005

Proactive Classroom Management. Louis G. Denti. Corwin, A Sage Publishing Company. 2012

The Behavior of Organisms, B. F. Skinner. The B. F. Skinner Foundation Publishing. 1999

The Best Classroom Management Practices for Reaching All Learners. Randi Stone. Corwin Press Books. 2004

The Classroom Survival Book (A Practical Manual For Teachers). Margaret Martin Maggs. Viewpoint, A Division of Franklin Watts, New York. 1980

The First Six Weeks of School / Edition. Center for Responsive Schools, Inc. 2015

The First Year Of Teaching (Real Stories from America's Teachers). Pearl Rock Kane. Walker Publishing Inc., USA. Thomas Allen & Sons, Canada. 1991

The New Teacher's Guide to Success: A personalized Planning Guide for Beginning Teachers. Matthew Haldeman. Shell Education. 2008

The Organized Teacher / Edition 2. Steve Springer, Brandy Alexander, Kimberly Persiani. McGraw-Hill Professional Publishing. 2011

The Special Educator's Toolkit: Everything You Need to Organize, Manage, and Monitor Your Classroom. Cindy, Ed. Golden Ed. Brookes. Paul H. Publishing Co. 2011

Tips From the Teachers (America's Best Describe Effective Classroom Methods). Charles S. Chase and Jacquline E. Chase. Technomic Publishing Co., Inc. Lancaster, Pennsylvania. USA. 1993

Understanding And Relating To Parents Professionally. Robert L. DeBruyn, (Author of The Master Teacher). The Master Teacher Inc., Publisher. Manhattan, Kansas, USA. 1986

What Great Teachers Do Differently. Todd Whitaker. Taylor & Francis. 2015

Will The Real Teacher Please Stand Up. R. Hawk Starkey, Ph. D. Inreach Publishing. Austin, TX. 1994

You Have to Go to School…You're the Teacher. Renee Rosenblum-Lowden. 2000

I hope that the information contained in this book will be of some assistance to you. It is not intended to replace any procedures given to you by your school system.

I would love to hear from you concerning your experiences and comments about this book. Write to us or visit our website at:

theKISSmethods@gmail.com

www.theKISSmethods.com

www.ingramcontent.com/pod-product-compliance
Lightning Source LLC
Chambersburg PA
CBHW080553170426
43195CB00016B/2772